About Mid
Wales

Ll
T

Lly
Cefnll

Powys

WITHDRAWN

37218 00265774 5

Published by Graffeg
First published 2007
Copyright © Graffeg 2007
ISBN 978 1 905582 05 1

Graffeg, Radnor Court, 256 Cowbridge
Road East, Cardiff CF5 1GZ Wales UK.
Tel: +44(0)29 2037 7312
sales@graffeg.com www.graffeg.com
Graffeg are hereby identified as the
authors of this work in accordance
with section 77 of the Copyrights,
Designs and Patents Act 1988.

Distributed by the Welsh Books
Council www.cllc.org.uk
castellbrychan@cllc.org.uk

A CIP Catalogue record for this book
is available from the British Library.

Designed and produced by
Peter Gill & Associates
sales@petergill.com
www.petergill.com

All rights reserved. No part of this
publication may be reproduced, stored
in a retrieval system or transmitted,
in any form or by any means,
electronic, mechanical, photocopying,
recording or otherwise, without the
prior permission of the publishers
Graffeg.

Map base information reproduced
by permission of Ordnance Survey
on behalf of HMSO
© Crown Copyright.
All rights reserved. Ordnance Survey
Licence number 100020518

About Mid Wales
Written by David Williams,
foreword by Siân Lloyd

The publishers are also grateful to
the Welsh Books Council for their
financial support and marketing
advice. www.gwales.com

Every effort has been made to
ensure that the information in this
book is current and it is given in good
faith at the time of publication. Please
be aware that circumstances can
change and be sure to check details
before making travel plans.

Front cover image: Llanidloes.

About Mid
Wales

Foreword

"Whether you live here or are visiting for
the first time, I hope that this book will
inspire you to explore Wales's many
cultural and historical treasures, leading
you to new and exciting experiences.
It is intended to be a source book of
ideas for things to do."

Wales is a remarkable part of the world where, over many centuries, people have created a rich and fascinating heritage. From battle-worn castles to settled towns and villages, from mines and quarries to elegant historic houses, there are tremendous places to visit.

Museums draw upon wonderful original material to tell our story. Many towns have local-history museums. The National Museum Wales, an impressive group of museums and galleries, illuminates our collective past through informative and innovative displays.

Our enthusiasm for culture, especially music and literature, is famous. Wales produces stars of concert hall, opera, stage, screen and rock arena – along with gifted writers and poets. There is strength in depth, from keen amateur activity in local halls and eisteddfodau to the thriving professional sphere. Major festivals, and smaller events, accommodate every cultural and artistic activity: music, literature, theatre, dance, the visual arts and others.

Wales asserts its cultural individuality in an increasingly interconnected and globalised world. The long history of the Welsh people has evolved into a forward-looking modern identity, based on respect for the past. As someone who works in both England and Wales, and travels widely, I enjoy sharing this distinctive sense of identity with people I meet.

I am fluently bilingual in Welsh and English and thank my parents for sending me to a Welsh school. The opportunities I received there – especially in public speaking, drama and music – set me on course to become a broadcaster.

The Welsh language, spoken by around half a million people, supports a wonderful literature and a thriving culture. English and Welsh enjoy official status together and many other languages are heard too, especially in the multicultural cities of Cardiff, Swansea and Newport.

Whether you live here or are visiting for the first time, I hope that this book will inspire you to explore Wales's many cultural and historic treasures. It is intended to be a source book of ideas for things to do. So, please enjoy the evocative photographs and learn interesting things but, above all, be sure to get out and about to experience the wonders of Wales for yourself.

Siân Lloyd

Above: **Brecon Jazz Festival.** One of Europe's largest jazz events, the Brecon Jazz Festival takes place each year close to the heart of the spectacular Brecon Beacons National Park.

Introduction

This book celebrates the historical and cultural attractions that make mid Wales such a special place. We hope that it will lead you to enjoyable discoveries and a deeper appreciation of this ancient and profoundly fascinating region and its people.

Located on the western side of the UK, Wales is bounded by the sea on three sides and shares a border with England to the east. Almost a quarter of its area enjoys special environmental designation.

Our three national parks – Snowdonia, the Brecon Beacons and the Pembrokeshire Coast – contain landscapes and habitats of international importance. Other regions throughout Wales are designated Areas of Outstanding Natural Beauty and there are more than 1,000 Sites of Special Scientific Interest.

But it is the way in which people have left their mark – on the landscape, in towns and cities, and on the world – that gives Wales its unique character. It is a place where a sense of history, and the achievements of the past, are valued by an advanced modern nation.

Wales is part of the United Kingdom and therefore is not fully a nation state. But its people certainly see themselves as a distinct nation. The Welsh language reinforces this identity, yet many people who do not speak it are also quick to assert their Welshness. The devolution of significant powers from Parliament in London to the National Assembly for Wales in Cardiff has given us one of the world's newest democratic institutions and greater autonomy.

Evidence of how people lived and worked over the centuries is preserved at our many ancient monuments, castles, historic houses and industrial locations. Wales has two UNESCO World Heritage Sites: the great medieval castles and town walls of north-west Wales and the industrial landscape of Blaenavon in the south-east.

Many places are in the care of either the National Trust or CADW, the Welsh Assembly Government's historic environment division. Museums and galleries, including the National Museum Wales, tell of our remarkable past.

The Welsh are seen as musically and lyrically gifted people. Ability in the areas is celebrated at local events and major festivals. The vigorous cultural life reflects the varied origins of the people (especially in the cities) and their typically open-minded gregariousness.

This book celebrates some of the historical and cultural attractions that make mid Wales such a special place. We hope that it will lead you to enjoyable discoveries and a deeper appreciation of this ancient and profoundly fascinating region and its people.

David Williams

Above: **National Eisteddfod.**
Held at the beginning of August, the National Eisteddfod moves to a different part of Wales each year.

About this book

The aim of this book is to give you a taste of some of the main cultural and historical attractions of mid Wales. It is one of a series of four regional pocket guides that cover, between them, the whole of Wales.

You will find information on many locations to visit and events to enjoy: castles, historic houses, industrial-heritage sites, museums, galleries, large festivals and local gatherings.

Each entry provides guidance on how to get there. Maps show the towns and villages mentioned, and the main roads. Contact information and website addresses will enable you to find current event programmes, opening times and any admission charges, and to plan your visit in detail.

We list the best-known attractions but, of course, Wales has such a rich heritage that there are many more places to explore. The main tourism websites – and those of organisations including CADW and the National Trust – are included here.

We also provide details of Tourism Information Centres, places to stay and eat, advice on mid Wales's public transport system and an introduction to the Welsh language. The book concludes with an index of places, attractions, festivals and events.

We hope you enjoy browsing in search of interesting places to visit and things to do.

Mid Wales
This region has isolated holy places, remote mineral mines and the wonderful coastline of Cardigan Bay.

Above left: **Powis Castle.** Powis Castle has medieval origins and contains some of the finest furniture and paintings in Wales – the views from its ornate terraces are tremendous.
Above right: **Hay-on-Wye.** This small town, on the border with England, grew around a Norman fortification. Full of bookshops, and famous as home to the Hay Festival, it attracts distinguished authors and thinkers each May, to celebrate literature and ideas.

Contents

Explore these elevated central regions of Wales with their green hills, dramatic mountains, fresh air and opportunities to relax or to be active. Visit traditional market towns, religious sites and places of industrial heritage. Go walking in the open spaces of the Brecon Beacons National Park or the Berwyn Hills. To the west is Ceredigion, with its heritage coastline and thriving centres of Welsh culture.

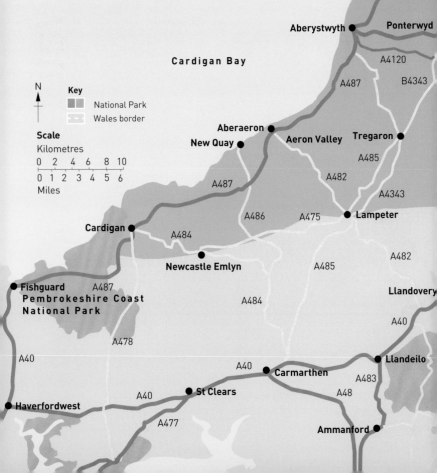

A496
A470
Dolgellau
A487
A493
Machynlleth

Aberystwyth **Ponterwyd**
Cardigan Bay
A4120
A487 B4343

N

Key
■■ National Park
⬚⬚ Wales border

Scale
Kilometres
0 2 4 6 8 10
0 1 2 3 4 5 6
Miles

Aberaeron
New Quay **Aeron Valley** **Tregaron**
A485
A482
A4343
A487
A486 A475 **Lampeter**
Cardigan
A484
A482
Newcastle Emlyn A485
Fishguard A487
Pembrokeshire Coast
National Park A484 **Llandovery**
A40
A478
A40 **Llandeilo**
A40 **Carmarthen** A483
A40 **St Clears** A48
Haverfordwest
A477 **Ammanford**

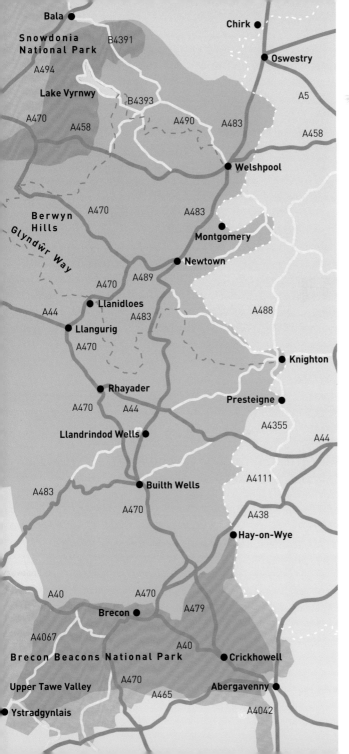

Bala ●
Chirk ●
Snowdonia
National Park
B4391
Oswestry ●
A494
A5
Lake Vyrnwy
B4393
A458
A470
A458
A490
A483
A458
Welshpool ●
A470
A483
Berwyn
Hills
Montgomery ●
Glyndŵr Way
Newtown ●
A470
A489
A488
A44
Llanidloes ●
A483
Llangurig ●
A470
Knighton ●
Rhayader ●
Presteigne ●
A470
A44
A4355
Llandrindod Wells ●
A44
A4111
Builth Wells ●
A483
A470
A438
Hay-on-Wye ●
A40
A470
A479
Brecon ●
A4067
A40
Brecon Beacons National Park
Crickhowell ●
A470
Upper Tawe Valley
Abergavenny ●
A465
● Ystradgynlais
A4042

Mid Wales

Mid Wales and the Brecon Beacons

Powis Castle, Presteigne Judges' Lodgings,
the Glyndŵr Way, Machynlleth, Crickhowell,
the Hay Literary Festival, the Brecon Jazz Festival,
Dan-yr-Ogof Caves, Craig-y-Nos, Llandrindod Wells
Victorian Festival, Llanwrtyd Wells bog snorkelling
and Mid Wales Opera.

Brecon

Among the most character -filled of Wales's market towns, Brecon's centre is a maze of narrow streets in which you will find shops – including some fine antique dealers – restaurants and ancient pubs. The town's Welsh name, Aberhonddu, estuary of the Honddu, reflects the fact that the town grew at the confluence of the rivers Honddu and Usk.

• The town centre streets are narrow and parking is scarce; use the signed car parks and enjoy exploring on foot.
www.exploremidwales.com

Brecon Cathedral. Following their conquest of Britain in 1066, the Normans quickly extended their influence into Wales.

At Brecon, Benedictine monks established a priory on the site of the existing church of St John. This flourished until the dissolution of the monasteries in 1537. Almost all of Brecon Cathedral dates from this original period. The building underwent major restoration in the 1860s under the direction of Sir Gilbert Scott. In 1923, as a result of the disestablishment of the Church in Wales in 1920, the Priory Church became the cathedral of the new diocese of Swansea and Brecon.

Above: **Waun Rydd.** Walking, climbing and pot-holing are popular in the Brecon Beacons. Call at the visitor centre, near Libanus, for details of outdoor activities.

Evening Meals

NITE
Jimmy Willies
SPOT
OPEN TILL 1
Free Entry
PROMOTIONS
Dance to the
sounds of 2day
FOOD AVAILABLE
Join in the fun @
Jimmy Willies

NTRANCE

THE
WHITE
HORSE
Breakfast & Bar Meals

Jimmy Willies
DOWNSTAIRS

• There is limited parking space at the cathedral, but a walk down from the town and along the river bank is enjoyable too.
Phone: 01874 623857
www.breconcathedral.org.uk

South Wales Borderers Museum. Military regalia collections reflect the history and character of a regiment that has existed for over 300 years – with Brecon being its base for 120 of them. The gun collection traces the evolution of weapons from the 18th century to the present day. The main attraction is the Zulu War room. The exploits of the 24th Regiment during the 1879 campaign are legendary and the film "Zulu" recreated the events surrounding the heroic defence of Rorke's Drift. The compelling story is made all the more real by the display of artefacts associated with the men who served there.
• A modest walk from the town centre, adjacent to the regimental barracks.
Phone: 01874 613310
www.rrw.org.uk

Theatr Brycheiniog. Wales is fortunate to have strong regional theatres and Theatr Brycheiniog is no exception. Since opening in 1997, it has established itself as a leading venue, presenting a diverse programme. It attracts some of the UK's top artists and companies, including The Royal National Theatre, the BBC National Orchestra of Wales, Northern Stage Ensemble, the Richard Alston Dance Company and household names in popular music, folk music and comedy. It enjoys a pleasant setting alongside the Monmouthshire and Brecon Canal (photo page 43).
• Event and performance details from the theatre or from the Tourist Information Centre.
Phone: 01874 611622
www.theatrbrycheiniog.co.uk

Builth Wells

For four days in July, this town on the bank of the river Wye becomes a focal point for the whole nation, as visitors, exhibitors and pampered animals converge on the **Royal Welsh Agricultural Show**. This celebration of the best of country life is a great day out for all the family. There's much to see in the main ring, including the parade of winning animals each afternoon, and the myriad displays and exhibition stands are a delight. Be sure also to pop into the **Wyeside Arts Centre**, near the bridge, to see what's on there.

Previous page: **Builth Wells The White Horse Pub.** The exterior of this pub is typical of the rustic charm found in Builth Wells.
Left: **Royal Welsh Agricultural Show.** One of the most prestigious events of its kind in Europe, the Royal Welsh Agricultural Show brings together the farming industry and the rural community in a celebration of the best of Welsh agriculture.

• Readily accessible along A-roads from all corners of Wales, as the varied accents of the farmers at the show will confirm.
www.builthwells.co.uk

....

Crickhowell

Delightfully situated where its fine stone-arched bridge crosses the river Usk, and surrounded by the distinctive ridged summits of the Black Mountains, Crickhowell is a pretty town blessed with some very agreeable pubs and restaurants. It is a perfect place, in fact, for a bracing walk followed by a leisurely meal. **The Bear Hotel** which retains the atmosphere of its days as a coaching inn, is especially popular.
• Six miles westward from Abergavenny, on the A40.
Phone: 01873 810408
www.bearhotel.co.uk

Tretower Court and Castle.
The stark 13th century keep of Tretower Castle stands on the remains of an earlier Norman earthwork and speaks eloquently of dangerous times. The charming manor house of Tretower Court, on the other hand, dates from the more settled 15th century, when its owners, the Vaughan family, felt secure enough to start building one of Wales's grandest medieval country residences. Open-air productions of Shakespeare are fittingly staged here

each summer.
• A mile or so along the A479 from its junction with the A40 north-west of Crickhowell, marked by a vintage AA phone box.
Phone: 01874 730279
www.cadw.wales.gov.uk

Hay-on-Wye

Famous as "The Town of Books", Hay-on-Wye has more than thirty bookshops which, along with the annual literary festival, have made this previously rather sleepy border town famous around the world. The region is immortalised in the diaries of Francis Kilvert, rector of nearby Clyro, who wrote sensitively of the life of an Anglican clergyman in this corner of rural Wales during late Victorian times.
• Right on the border with England, on the A438 north-east of Brecon.
www.exploremidwales.com

Previous page: **Brecon.** At one end of the Monmouthshire & Brecon Canal lies the historic market town of Brecon where the narrow streets and passageways are lined with Georgian and Jacobean shopfronts.
Above left: **Hay-on-Wye.** If you've been trying to track down an out-of-print book, or if you would like to relive the magic of a childhood favourite, the knowledgeable bookshop owners of Hay-on-Wye are likely to be able to help.
Above: **The Bear Hotel.** This former coaching inn as as popular today as it was in the days of horse-drawn transport.

Knighton

This attractive town is home to an interactive exhibition describing the history, flora and fauna of Offa's Dyke, the earthwork that has more or less marked the border between Wales and England since Saxon times.

The Offa's Dyke Path national trail extends 177 miles (285km) from the mouth of the Wye at Sedbury, near Chepstow, northward to Prestatyn in Flintshire, with Knighton at about the halfway point.

• On the A488, some eighteen miles north-east of Llandrindod Wells.
www.exploremidwales.com

Glyndŵr Way National Trail.
This 132-mile route links many locations associated with Owain Glyndŵr's campaigns for Welsh independence. From Sycharth near Welshpool, where the hospitality of his court was legendary, to the borderlands around Knighton, the path passes through areas where he fought many battles and generated unshakeable loyalty.

• Obtain detailed maps and guidebooks from Tourist Information Centres and local bookshops.

The Thomas Shop, Penybont
In this age of standardised high street stores and supermarkets this authentic village store is a real education for younger visitors.

Dating back to 1805, the Thomas Shop was the socio-economic centre for the area before the steam trains led to the development of the Victorian town of Llandrindod Wells just five miles away. In the shop you will find the shelves brimming with items that celebrate the period of time when the shop was active as both a drapery and grocery store. The Thomas Shop is not just a museum, on the shelves there are many items for sale, including beautiful Welsh Throws and other Welsh textile crafts, as well as grocery items such as the now famous Thomas Shop marmalades and jams.

• Penybont is situated where the A488 south of Knighton meets the A44.
www.thomas-shop.com

Llanidloes

Four streets meet at the black-and-white timbered market hall, built on wooden stilts, in this attractive town centre. An exhibition about timber-framed buildings is open throughout the year. The museum of local history tells the story of agriculture, mining, and the rise

---

Previous page: **Hay-on-Wye.** Sitting at the north-eastern corner of the Brecon Beacons National Park, on the border with England, Hay-on-Wye has a colourful history and seems distanced from the trappings of the 21st century.
Above: **The Glyndŵr Way.** One of numerous well-signed routes passing through historic regions of Wales.

of nonconformism and Chartism in the region.
• South-west of Newtown, on the main A470 road that runs the length of Wales.
www.llanidloes.com

Minerva Arts Centre. The woollen industry, which was important to the economy of this region for centuries, has a shop window at the Minerva Arts Centre. Here, at the home of the Quilt Association, you will discover displays of antique quilts, including styles produced in Wales over the past two centuries, as well as the frames, templates and other equipment with which they were made. The centre also hosts workshops, lectures and courses.
• In the centre of Llanidloes.

Phone: 01686 413467
www.quilt.org.uk

Llanwrtyd Wells

Let's just say that here, in a place that describes itself as "The Wackiest Town in Britain", you are likely to encounter some pretty unusual goings-on. We're not talking ancient traditions here. It was the local pub landlord, Gordon Green MBE, who enriched the world by devising the sport of **bog-snorkelling**, along with a series of other distinctive events. These include the **Man versus Horse Marathon**, **the Morris in the Forest folk dancing festival**, and the **Real Ale Wobble** – a two day mountain-biking and beer drinking festival.

• Between Builth Wells and Llandovery, on the A483.
www.exploremidwales.com

Machynlleth

Machynlleth occupies a special place in Welsh history, as centre of the revolution by which Owain Glyndŵr reasserted Welsh identity at the beginning of the 15th century. The building believed to have been used for his parliament of 1404 still stands. The busy main street has attractive shops and pubs, overlooked by an impressive Gothic Revival clocktower. The Tabernacle, a former Wesleyan chapel, houses the **Museum of Modern Art Wales**, with its excellent auditorium,

recording studio, exhibition spaces, artists' studios and rehearsal rooms. It is the main venue for the **Machynlleth Festival** which is held in late August.

Previous page: **Llanidloes.** The timbered buildings of the town square and China Street lend a quaint dignity to the attractive centre of Llanidloes.
Above left: **Machynlleth.** The most prominent feature in Machynlleth is the 19th century clocktower, nearly 80 feet tall. From here the three main streets radiate, making it the hub of the town.
Above right: **Monmouthshire and Brecon Canal.** Originally built to serve industry, many of Wales's historic canals and railways may be enjoyed under more leisurely circumstances today.

• From the clocktower, **The Tabernacle** is a short walk along the road towards Dolgellau, and the parliament building is along the main street, on the left.
Phone: 01654 703355
(The Tabernacle)
www.momawales.org.uk

Museum of Mechanical Magic, Llanbrynmair. This collection of moving figures, mechanical toys and automata, all of which display superb craftsmanship, will amuse and entertain visitors of all ages. Open all year, it also features a giant moving dragon, a rabbit village, the Timberkits factory, a shop and a café.
• Between Machynlleth and Caersws, on the A470.
Phone: 01650 511514

Montgomery

This beautifully picturesque border town is set around a central square, where the petite town hall and the distinguished architecture of the houses make you feel as if you are on the set of a historical drama.
• South of Welshpool along B-roads from Garthmyl or Kingswood.
www.exploremidwales.com

Newtown

Occupying a strategic position at a bridging point on the river Severn, Newtown is a busy centre of local government and commerce. Highlights include

the **Robert Owen** and **WH Smith museums**, **Theatr Hafren**, the contemporary **Oriel Davies Gallery** and the **Textile Museum**, which celebrates the region's woollen and flannel industry. The world's first mail-order shopping service – Pryce-Jones, which listed Queen Victoria amongst its customers – operated from the large red -brick warehouse that still overlooks the town.

• There's a large car park off the A489.

www.exploremidwales.com

Mid Wales Opera. Founded in 1988, the award-winning Mid Wales Opera has established itself as one of the UK's foremost touring opera companies.

Its productions have been performed in over eighty venues in the UK and Ireland. From the elegant Opera House at Buxton, and Aldeburgh's Snape Maltings, to the intimate theatre at

---

Above left: **Montgomery Castle.** The hilltop site of Montgomery Castle was chosen for its defensive advantages, including the wide views over the surrounding countryside, which may be enjoyed under more peaceful circumstances today.

Above right: **Bog-snorkelling.** If you can find the motivation to submerge yourself in the cold brown waters of the bog-snorkelling course at Llanwrtyd Wells, and power your way to the finish in a winning time, you will have a great story to tell for many years to come!

Felin-Fach, Lampeter, the company's annual visit is eagerly anticipated by opera lovers throughout the country.

• You will find the programme in local papers, from Tourist Information Centres and via a link from the Arts Council of Wales website.
Phone: 01938 500611
www.midwalesopera.co.uk

Presteigne

This fascinating little town sits on the border between Wales and Herefordshire. Its half-timbered buildings date from the 14th century. Enter the fascinating world of Victorian judges, their servants and their felonious guests as you explore the cells, courtroom and living quarters of the **Judges' Lodgings**, the town's award-winning, hands-on family museum.

• Travel eastward from Llandrindod Wells on the A44 and B4362.
Phone: 01544 260650 (TIC)
www.judgeslodging.org.uk

Upper Tawe Valley

Dan-yr-Ogof Caves. The emergence of the River Llynfell from a cave was a mystery to local people until, in 1912, Tommy and Jeff Morgan found the courage to explore further. Using only candles to light their way, and arrows in the sand to find their way back, they discovered a wonderland of stalactites and stalagmites. When they found an underground lake, deep inside the mountain, they returned with coracles and sculled across not just one lake, but four. Since then cavers have found over ten miles (16km) of amazing caves. The journey through the illuminated Dan-yr-Ogof Caves is an experience you will never forget. On the surface, the Shire Horse Centre, farm, museum and life-sized dinosaurs will make your visit complete.

• From J43 on the M4, the A465 north-eastward to the A4221 and A4067 combines speed and scenery. Phone: 01639 730284
www.showcaves.co.uk

Craig-y-Nos. This early Victorian country house in the upper Swansea Valley was bought in 1878 by the opera singer Adelina Patti, who could fairly be

---

Previous page: **Dan-yr-Ogof Caves.** The underground tour of the Dan-yr-Ogof Caves is memorable; the occasional concerts held there equally so.
Above right: **Montgomery.** In 1086, Roger, Earl of Shrewsbury, built a small castle here, to guard a strategically important ford across the River Severn – and named it Montgomery, after his home in Normandy.
Below right: **Montgomery Canal.** The canal is a haven for wildlife with many Sites of Special Scientific Interest and offers many opportunities for walkers, canoeists and anglers.

described as an international superstar of her day. She created a stylish retreat where she could recharge her energy between tours. This was one of the first private homes in Britain to have electricity, which enabled Adelina to install the latest lighting technology in her theatre.

An electric Orchestrion organ – driven by that early form of digital music, punched paper rolls – was also acquired. Following dedicated fundraising and restoration efforts, Craig-y-Nos is now a hotel, and the beautiful theatre hosts regular recitals and concerts.

☙ Near the Dan-yr-Ogof Caves on the A4067.
Phone: 01639 730205
www.craigynoscastle.co.uk

Welshpool

This bustling market town serves a large agricultural hinterland and has the largest sheep market in Europe. It is a pleasant walk from the town centre to Powis Castle, through parkland designed by Capability Brown. Or stroll along the towpath of the **Montgomery Canal** to the **Powysland Museum**, where you will learn about the Stone Age inhabitants, Roman settlement, Viking attacks and the growth of Christianity in the area. Allow plenty of time to explore both Powis Castle and the town, with its broad main thoroughfare.
• www.exploremidwales.com

Powis Castle. Originally a fortress of the Welsh Princes of Powys, and built around 1200, this sumptuous castle was remodelled over four centuries by the Herbert family. Its outstandingly fine gardens – laid out in French and Italian styles and overhung with enormous clipped yew trees – shelter rare and tender plants, including grapevines. The castle contains historically important furniture and paintings. Treasures from India are displayed in the **Clive Museum** – Edward, son of Robert Clive of India, married Lady Henrietta Herbert in 1784.

• Prominently signed from the A458 and A483 south-west of Welshpool. Phone: 01938 551929 www.nationaltrust.org.uk

Welshpool and Llanfair Light Railway. One of Wales's "Great Little Railways", this narrow-gauge steam railway runs between Welshpool and Llanfair Caereinion, through the glorious countryside of the Banwy valley.

Previous page and above left: **Powis Castle.** Most of the great Welsh castles were allowed to decay when the medieval wars ended, but Powis survives as a captivating example of a preserved military stronghold. This statue of a shepherd merrily playing a flute looks out over the fine gardens of Powis Castle.
Above right: **Lake Vyrnwy.** The Sculpture Trail at Lake Vyrnwy is a visual and tactile delight – huge blocks of timber have been carved and assembled in ways that will stimulate and provoke.

• Llanfair Caereinion is nine miles west of Welshpool, on the A458. Phone: 01938 810441
www.wllr.org.uk

Sculpture Trail at Lake Vyrnwy.
Each summer for several years beginning in 1999, sculptors from countries all over northern Europe, including Scandinavia, the Baltic States and Russia, gathered at Lake Vyrnwy for an international symposium. The results of their efforts form the Lake Vyrnwy Sculpture Trail, spectacularly positioned below the dam of this enormous reservoir, which has more than sixty works skilfully shaped from local pine. These fill the available space at Lake Vyrnwy but the tradition continues in new locations around mid Wales.
• The B4393 from Llanfyllin meanders around the far end of the lake and back.
Phone: 01691 870278
www.waterscape.com

**Pererindod Melangell –
Melangell's Pilgrimage.**
Saint Melangell is the Welsh patron saint of animals. She achieved this distinction when, on seeing a local prince and his huntsmen chasing some hares, she sheltered the animals under her cloak and charmed the prince into abandoning his pursuit.
A walking trail in the upper Vyrnwy and Tanat valleys takes you through idyllic countryside – of precisely the sort you would imagine as the setting for the enchanting story – and past the remote church of the kindly saint at Pennant Melangell.
• Start at Pont Llogel, off the B4395, just below Lake Vyrnwy. The walk is a 15-mile one-way trek, finishing in Llangynog, sign posted with waymarkers. The going is easy along the first half, then becomes more challenging.

Festivals and events

Hay Festival of Literature.
Near the end of **May** each year, the population of this small border town increases dramatically as famous authors and celebrities, and thousands of devoted readers of their books, gather for this annual banquet of literary delights. The prodigious events programme includes talks and interviews in the festival's marquees, followed by signings in the on-site bookshop and an impressive choice of spoken, dramatic and musical entertainment each evening.

Previous page: **Brecon Jazz Festival.** The friendly atmosphere is generated as much in the streets and open spaces of the town as in the concerts given by jazz legends in concert venues.
Right: **Theatr Brycheiniog.** Since opening ten years ago Theatr Brycheiniog has established itself as one of the leading venues in Wales attracting some of the UK's leading performing artists and companies.

• The good humour of staff manning temporary car parks eases your arrival.
Phone: 0870 990 1299
www.hayfestival.com

Brecon Jazz Festival. There's something about jazz, especially when played in the open air, that lifts the spirits. Every **August**, top performers in all styles of jazz bring their sounds to the main square, market hall, car parks, **Theatr Brycheiniog** and hotels of Brecon, for one of the UK's best jazz festivals.
• Be prepared to park some distance away and to be on your feet – spectating or dancing – as the music exerts its magic.
Phone: 01874 625511
www.breconjazz.co.uk

Llandrindod Wells. Towards the end of **August**, the dignified streets and handsome gardens of Llandrindod Wells celebrate the town's origins as a 19th century spa resort. Residents and visitors alike dress up to enjoy themed events, including street theatre, music-hall performances and traditional sports and games. Don't miss the funfair, food and craft stalls and the elegant **Pump Rooms** – where you may partake of afternoon tea to the accompaniment of congenial music.
• On the A483 north of Builth Wells, with broad streets and ample parking.
www.llandrindod.co.uk

Presteigne Music Festival.
Founded in 1983 this annual gathering in **August** has a reputation for excellence. It attracts performers and composers of distinction and has received glowing endorsements in the music media, including BBC Radio 3. It organises workshop sessions in local schools, at which professional musicians inspire children with performances of classical music, and it is especially known for nurturing talented performers early in their careers.
• Phone: 01544 267800
www.presteignefestival.com

The Green Man Festival.
This three-day gathering each

August features musicians of the stature of Donovan, Robert Plant, Joanna Newsom and Bert Jansch, along with a spectrum of alternative folk, experimental and psychedelic performers from Wales and beyond. Other attractions include DJ stages, films, literary and science tents. A related event, 'The Rite of Spring', is held at Baskerville House in the Black Mountains around the spring equinox, 21 March.
• The festival is held at Glanusk Park Estate, situated in the Usk Valley, Crickhowell.
www.thegreenmanfestival.co.uk

Above: **Hay Festival.** One of the largest literary festivals in the world and a great place to bump into celebrities or your favourite author.

45

Ceredigion

Aberystwyth, Llywernog silver and lead mine museum, Strata Florida Abbey, Lampeter, the Vale of Rheidol Railway, Llanerchaeron, Cardigan, the Aberystwyth Arts Centre, the National Library of Wales and the Tregaron Welsh Gold Centre.

Aberaeron

Once a small fishing village, Aberaeron grew (following the creation of its harbour between 1807 and 1811) into one of the major trading and shipbuilding ports of Cardigan Bay. With the expansion of the harbour came the expansion of local enterprise; the site of the local woollen mill still stands and the ironworks produced the famous Aberaeron shovel. Today the town is still a focal point for local communities but the main industry is now tourism.

The Harbourmaster Hotel at Aberaeron, where the eponymous official once trained his telescope on ships sailing in, has stylishly contemporary interiors and an imaginative menu based on fine local produce such as Cardigan Bay crab and lobster, and Aberaeron mackerel. The Harbourmaster is a Grade II listed building, dating back to 1811.
Phone: 01545 570755
www.harbour-master.com

Aberystwyth

The university town of **Aberystwyth** grew from a small settlement guarded by one of the first of Edward I's castles, built in 1277, which stands ruined on its

Above: **Aberystwyth**. The coastal path above Aberystwyth provides spectacular views of the town.

breezy promontory overlooking the bay. Inland, Llanbadarn Fawr, its church austerely spiritual in the Celtic fashion, is where the 6th century scholar-saint Padarn founded his monastery. During the 19th century, the harbour handled lead and zinc from mines in the hills, and general cargo from around the Irish Sea.

With the arrival of the railway in 1864, the town became a popular seaside resort. The wide promenade and the railway to the top of Constitution Hill still attract the crowds.

• The A470 and A44, from the direction of Newtown, take you across the bare terrain of the Cambrian mountains.
www.aberystwyth-online.co.uk

National Library of Wales.
Overlooking the town from its commanding hilltop site, Aberystwyth's eyrie of erudition is one of the great libraries of the world. Since 1911, it has enjoyed the right to acquire a free copy of every printed work published in Britain and Ireland. It holds a huge collection of works about Wales and the other Celtic countries, in the form of books and pamphlets, magazines and newspapers, microforms, ephemera and a wealth of digital material. Thousands of manuscripts and archives, pictures and photographs, maps, sound recordings and moving images are available for research, and there are many treasures on public display. 'The Drwm', a

multi-media auditorium, brings the library's rich collections to life in new ways that enthuse and involve its visitors. The varied programme includes musical and theatrical performances, book launches, lectures and world-class films. The library also arranges exhibitions throughout the year.

• There is parking near the library, which can be seen for miles around, and there are regular buses up the steep hill to the university campus.
Phone: 01970 632800
www.llgc.org.uk

Aberystwyth Arts Centre.

The award-winning Aberystwyth Arts Centre is among the largest and busiest in Wales, with a wide-ranging programme of events and activities across all art forms. It welcomes over 500,000 visitors a year, including over 70,000

Previous page and above left: **The Harbourmaster Hotel.** Occupies the building from which Aberaeron's harbourmaster once trained his telescope on ships sailing in.
Above right: **Aberystwyth Arts Centre.** The award-winning Arts Centre has a wide-ranging programme of events and activities across all art forms.
Next page: **National Library of Wales, Aberystwyth.** The library has many rare books, including the first book printed in Welsh (from 1546) and the first Welsh translation of the Bible (1588). It also has the earliest surviving manuscript entirely in Welsh, The Black Book of Carmarthen.

Eryri
Snowdonia

participants in its community arts and education programme. It is a department of the University of Wales, Aberystwyth, and sits at the heart of the university campus.

• As part of the spacious campus, access and parking are straightforward.
Phone: 01970 623232
www.aberystwythartscentre.co.uk

Vale of Rheidol Railway.
The gleaming steam trains of this preserved narrow-gauge railway huff and puff their way up the twisting valley of the river Rheidol from Aberystwyth's main station to picturesque **Pontarfynach**, or **Devil's Bridge**. The hugely appealing scenery belies the industrial purpose of the line,

which opened in 1902 to serve the nearby lead mines, though passengers and timber also became mainstays of its traffic.

• Enjoyable signposted walks radiate from the vicinity of the falls at Devil's Bridge.
Phone: 01970 625819
www.rheidolrailway.co.uk

Ceredigion Museum.
This informative museum is attractively housed in the former Coliseum theatre and cinema. Its displays cover the rich history of this fascinating and largely rural region of Wales: they highlight the significance of agriculture, seafaring and lead mining. There is also a gallery displaying a changing programme of visual art.

• There is usually parking space along the promenade, giving a good excuse to explore the nearby town centre on foot.
Phone: 01970 633088
www.ceredigion.gov.uk

Constitution Hill. For spectacular views over Cardigan Bay and much of Ceredigion, take the cliff railway to the 430-foot (131m) summit of Aberystwyth's Constitution Hill, at the northern end of the promenade. Originally operated by means of a water-balanced funicular system, the railway was equipped with electric winding equipment in 1921. The Camera Obscura projects images of the bay, the town and the surrounding countryside onto a large white table; it opened in 1985 as a reconstruction of a popular Victorian attraction.
• The lower station is located just behind the terraced boarding houses and hotels of the promenade.
www.aberystwyth-online.co.uk

Aeron Valley

Llanerchaeron. Set in beautiful Dyffryn Aeron, the Aeron valley,

Above left: **Aberystwyth Arts Centre.** National Youth Theatre of Wales production of Whisper in the Woods.
Above right: **Aberystwyth's Constitution Hill.** The summit offers tremendous views over Aberystwyth and across Cardigan Bay to the Llŷn Peninsula and Pembrokeshire.

this fine house has altered little since it was designed by John Nash in the 1790s. It is the most complete example of his early work. This was a self-sufficient estate, with home farm, dairy, laundry, brewery and salting house. Today it is a working organic farm, producing home-grown produce.

• Two miles inland from Aberaeron, on the A482.
Phone: 01545 570200
www.nationaltrust.org.uk

Cardigan

Cardigan – Aberteifi. It was here in 1176, in the castle overlooking the river, that Lord Rhys ap Gruffudd – premier among regional Welsh rulers at the time – held what is regarded as the first national eisteddfod. The tradition grew whereby the best poets and musicians of the day were rewarded by being invited to a chair at the top table, an honour echoed in today's eisteddfod chairing ceremony. At nearby St Dogmael's, the church contains the 6th century Sagranus stone which – by commemorating the Irish ruler buried there in both Latin and the ancient Ogham script – made possible the deciphering of the early Irish language. Cardigan is an important place of pilgrimage for the Roman Catholic church; the national shrine of Wales is at the church of Our Lady of the Taper.

• This important regional centre

has a thriving high street, which fills with stalls for the traditional fair each November.
www.visitcardigan.com
(photo page 60)

Cardigan Heritage Centre.
Visit this 18th century warehouse on the bank of the river Teifi to learn all about the history of Cardigan. The town has many places of historical interest including the **castle**, **priory**, **Shire Hall**, **Guildhall** and several **churches**. One of the Russian guns faced by the Light Brigade of the 11th Hussars as they made their disastrous charge at Balaclava during the Crimean War, under the command of the Earl of Cardigan, stands outside the Guildhall.
• Local guidebooks and leaflets are available from the Tourist Information Centre and the excellent local shops.
Phone: 01239 614404
www.ceredigion.gov.uk

Theatr Mwldan. Established in
1983 by Cardigan Theatre, a local amateur company, this thriving theatre has grown, following a £7 million development project, into a multi-purpose centre for the arts. It has two theatres, a rehearsal studio and a visual arts exhibition space, along with excellent front-of-house and

Above: **Llanerchaeron.**
The domestic amenities necessary to keep a busy late-18th century household running smoothly are an especially fascinating feature of Llanerchaeron.

dining amenities. More than five thousand people pass through its doors each week.
• Call in for a programme and inspect whatever is on in the exhibition gallery.
Phone: 01239 621200
www.mwldan.co.uk

Lampeter

Lampeter is home to the oldest college of the University of Wales: its specialisation in religious studies and the liberal arts dates back to 1822. To the north-east, on the scenic B4343 towards Tregaron, is **Llanddewi Brefi** where you will find a church dedicated to David, the patron saint of Wales. It was here that the ground is said to have risen beneath his feet, so that he could be better seen and heard by his eager congregation.
• Some twenty-eight miles south of Aberystwyth, along the A485.
www.tourism.ceredigion.gov.uk

Theatr Felinfach. Many visiting companies are amazed to see a fully equipped theatre here in the far west of Wales, and to see it brimming with life. They quickly realise that the theatre's strength derives from its solid foundations in the region's vibrant Welsh-language culture, and that it belongs to people of all age groups and backgrounds.
• At Felinfach in the Aeron valley (A482) between Lampeter and Aberaeron.
Phone: 01570 470697
www.ceredigion.gov.uk

Teifi Valley Railway. Created
from a branch of the Great
Western Railway, this short but
scenic line offers splendid views
of the beautiful Teifi valley and
a nostalgic reminder of the days
of steam. With unspoilt woodland
to either side, the train passes
ancient stone workings along the
route of an ancient drovers' trail
as it follows the bank of the Teifi.
You may disembark and watch
the crew as they uncouple the
engine and move it to the front
of the train for your return
journey. Back in the station
yard at Henllan, you can get
a refreshing cup of tea and a
sandwich in the tea room.
• Henllan is a couple of miles
east of Newcastle Emlyn, on
the A484.

Phone: 01559 371077
www.teifivalleyrailway.com

New Quay

With its picturesque houses,
pubs and restaurants clinging
to the hills above the blue waters

Previous page: **Cardigan Heritage
Centre.** Trace the history of
Cardigan from pre-Norman times
to the present day at this Grade II
listed building. The Cardigan
Heritage Centre also houses
changing exhibitions on local
themes, a craft and book
shop and a riverside café.
Above: **Cardigan.** An ancient Welsh
cultural and commercial centre on
the Teifi estuary, now a thriving
market town famous for its food
festival and autumn fair.

of Cardigan Bay, this small port and seaside resort has great character. During its 19th century heyday as a shipbuilding centre, some 250 sailing vessels – sloops, smacks, ketches and schooners – were launched here.
• From the A487 at Synod Inn, between Cardigan and Aberaeron, take the A486.
www.tourism.ceredigion.gov.uk

Ponterwyd

Llywernog Silver and Lead Mine Museum. Head inland from Aberystwyth and you will soon find yourself enjoying remarkable vistas of stark moorland above snug green valleys. The Automobile Association has described the B4574 through Cwm Ystwyth as one of the ten most scenic drives in the world. Hereabouts, in conditions that make you marvel at their toughness, people once mined a range of metal ores, including rock containing the precious silver that was made into coins at a Royal Mint in Aberystwyth.
• The Llywernog Mining Museum is off the A44 near Ponterwyd. Phone: 01970 890620
www.silverminetours.co.uk

Tregaron

The Welsh Gold Centre and Gallery. On the square in Tregaron, you will find a fine statue of **Henry Richard MP** – local chapel stalwart, secretary

of the Peace Society and early advocate of a League of Nations. Nearby is The Welsh Gold Centre, the premises of Rhiannon Jewellery, where you may watch the jeweller and her staff working gold and silver into intricate designs, many of them inspired by Celtic art and legend. Work by artists in a range of materials is shown in the centre's gallery and shop.

• On the A485, eleven miles north-east of Lampeter, eighteen miles south-east of Aberystwyth. Phone: 01974 298415
www.rhiannon.co.uk

Strata Florida Abbey. Standing serenely in its remote valley, the 12th century Cistercian abbey of Strata Florida – Vale of Flowers –

was an important religious house and an influential centre of Welsh culture, patronised by princes and poets. Dafydd ap Gwilym, the greatest of Welsh medieval poets, is commemorated here. The Romanesque west doorway, the abbey's most striking feature, frames the hills where the monks once farmed. The south transept

Previous page: **New Quay.** The narrow streets that rise from the harbour at New Quay are permeated by a tangible sense of the history of this attractive seaport village.
Above left: **The Welsh Gold Centre.** View an ever-changing display of paintings and craft items at this bright and airy exhibition gallery in Tregaron.
Above right: **Strata Florida.** A monastic community founded in 1164.

features fine medieval floor tiles.
• Turn off the B4343 at
Pontrhydfendigaid, five miles
north-east of Tregaron.
Phone: 01974 831261
www.cadw.wales.gov.uk

Festivals and events

Aberystwyth MusicFest.
A glittering line-up of celebrated
artists leads a programme of the
highest quality music-making
and teaching at Aberystwyth's
International Festival and
Summer School each **July**.
The shared enjoyment of
audience, student and artist
creates a refreshing and
inspirational community
atmosphere.
• The websites of the Arts
Council of Wales and Cerdd
Ystwyth (Aberystwyth's music
shop) carry authoritative
programmes.
www.aberystwythartscentre.co.uk
/musicfest

Cardigan River and Food Festival.
An annual event that
celebrates the River Teifi and
the diversity of food grown and
prepared in the area. A one-day
event, held in mid **August**, the
festival boasts a variety of food
stalls, cooking demonstrations,
river activities and boat races.
• Contact: Matthew Newbold.
Phone: 01239 615554
www.visitcardigan.com/cardigan-
festivals-river-food.shtm

Cardigan Bay Seafood Festival.
Held on the quaysides around

Aberaeron's picturesque harbour each **July**, this is where to sample mouth-watering local fish and shellfish. There are mackerel barbecues, crab-picking and catching competitions, whelk racing, brass bands, jazz, shanty singers and beach art.
• Contact: Harbourmaster Hotel Phone: 01545 570755

Aberystwyth and Ceredigion County Show.
Held at the Gelli Angharad fields every **June**, this enjoyable agricultural show attracts visitors from all over Ceredigion and beyond. The main elements are the livestock competitions (including categories for horses, cattle and poultry) and the popular dog shows.

• Phone: 01974 298 367
www.aberystwythshow.com

Aberystwyth Farmers' Market.
This is one of the largest farmers' markets Wales, hosting up to 30 stalls on the first and third Saturdays each month, at Aberystwyth's North Parade. There is a wide range of produce (including organic), plants and craft items.
• Phone: 01970 633066

Above left: **Cardigan Bay Seafood Festival.** Held in mid July when the local catch is plentiful.
Above right: **Aberystwyth Farmers' Market.** Open air stalls sell a wide range of fresh, local produce.
Next page: **Aberystwyth and Ceredigion County Show.** One of the many equestrian events at the Show.

Where to eat and stay

Alphabetical listing with contact details of restaurants and accommodation

Bear Hotel*, Crickhowell
Phone: 01873 810408
www.bearhotel.co.uk

Carlton House*, Llanwrtyd Wells
Phone: 01591 610248
www.carltonrestaurant.co.uk

Conrah*, Nr Aberystwyth
Phone: 01970 617941
www.conrah.co.uk

Harbourmaster*, Aberaeron
Phone: 01545 570755
www.harbour-master.com

Hive on the Quay, Aberaeron
Phone: 01545 570445
www.hiveonthequay.co.uk

Lake Country House*,
Llangammarch Wells
Phone: 01591 620202
www.lakecountryhouse.co.uk

Lake Vyrnwy Hotel*, Llanwddyn
Phone: 01691 870692
www.lakevyrnwy.com

Llangoed Hall*, Llyswen
Phone: 01874 754525
www.llangoedhall.com

Nantyffin Cider Mill, Crickhowell
Phone: 01873 810775
www.cidermill.co.uk

Milebrook House*, Knighton
Phone: 01547 528632
www.milebrookhouse.co.uk

Penbontbren*, Nr Cardigan
Phone: 01239 810248
www.penbontbren.com

Seeds, Llanfyllin
Phone: 01691 648604

Talkhouse*, Pontdolgoch
Phone: 01686 688919
www.talkhouse.co.uk

Tipple 'n' Tiffin, Brecon
Phone: 01874 611866
www.brycheiniog.co.uk

Waterdine*, Llanfair
Phone: 01547 528214
www.waterdine.com

West Arms*, Nr Llangollen
Phone: 01691 600665
www.thewestarms.co.uk

Wynnstay*, Machynlleth
Phone: 01654 702941
www.wynnstay-hotel.com

Ynyshir Hall*, Nr Machynlleth
Phone: 01654 781209
www.ynyshir-hall.co.uk

* Accommodation available

Information and useful websites

Tourist Information Centres throughout Wales have expert and welcoming staff who can offer independent assistance with planning routes, booking accommodation and the search for information on places or events to visit. They are your one-stop shop for holiday and short-break information, late availability and last-minute offers.

For a full list of Tourist Information Centres www.visitwales.com

Tourist Information Centres:
Mid Wales and the Brecon Beacons
T 01874 622485

Ceredigion – Cardigan Bay
T 01239 613230

Useful websites

Castles and heritage:
www.cadw.wales.gov.uk
www.nationaltrust.org.uk
www.bbc.co.uk/wales/history
(BBC Wales)
www.llgc.org.uk
(National Library of Wales)

Museums and galleries:
www.museumwales.ac.uk

Festivals and events:
www.eisteddfod.org.uk
(the National Eisteddfod of Wales)
www.urdd.org/eisteddfodau/2007
(Urdd Youth Eisteddfod)
www.artswales.org.uk
(Arts Council of Wales)
www.cerddystwyth.co.uk (festivals
list by Aberystwyth music shop)
www.victorianfestival.co.uk
(Llandrindod Wells)
www.hayfestival.co.uk
(Hay Festival of Literature)
www.rwas.co.uk
(Royal Welsh Show)
www.breconjazz.co.uk
(Brecon Jazz Festival)
www.thingstodo.org.uk
www.llanwrtyd-wells.powys.org.uk
www.homecomingwales.com
(choir listings)

Other websites
www.ccw.gov.uk (National Trails)
www.breconbeacons.org
(Brecon Beacons National Park)

How to get here

By car. The UK's road network serves visitors to Wales well, making it easy to get to by car. The M4 connects mid Wales to the M6 and beyond.

By train. Wales is easy to get to from all of the UK. From London Euston there is a service that will take you to Newtown in three and a half hours, with one change via Birmingham.

It also takes around three hours to get from Manchester to the town of Llandudno on Wales's north coast.

If you are visiting from overseas you will find that there are good links between all major airports and the main rail network. For rail enquiries and booking ring + 44(0) 8457 48 49 50 or visit one of the following websites: www.nationalrail.co.uk, www.thetrainline.com or www.qjump.co.uk

By coach or bus. National Express offers a nationwide service of fast, reliable express coaches. There is a good service from London Victoria coach station to many towns and cities in Wales as well as from many cities and towns in both England and Scotland. For example, the journey time between London and Aberystwyth is around seven hours. There are also convenient Flightlink coach services from major airports to destinations in Wales. For information and bookings call + 44 (0) 8705 808080 or go to: www.nationalexpress.co.uk Inside Wales there is an extensive network of regional and local bus services.

By air. There are regular direct flights to Cardiff International Airport from a wide range of destinations, including Amsterdam, Cork, Glasgow, London City, Paris and Prague. Also, Amsterdam, Dublin and Paris act as gateway hubs for European and international flights. For flight information call +44 (0) 1446 711111 email infodesk@cwl.aero or visit www.cial.co.uk London's airports and those at Birmingham and Manchester are all good gateways to Wales. Each has good road and rail connections.

By sea. Three ferry companies operate services between South West Wales and Ireland. They are: **Irish Ferries.** Rosslare to Pembroke. Tel: +44 (0) 8705 171717 www.irishferries.com **Stena Line.** Rosslare to Fishgard. Tel: +44 (0) 8705 707070 www.stenaline.co.uk **Swansea-Cork ferries.** Cork to Swansea. Tel: +44 (0) 1792 456116 www.swanseacorkferries.com

Other ferry ports (along England's south coast and elsewhere) have good cross-country motorway and main road links to Wales. For car travellers arriving on the EuroTunnel service it is motorway all the way from Dover to Wales.

Castles and heritage throughout Wales

Most of the many archaeological sites, castles and historic houses of Wales, and numerous former centres of industry, are in the care of one of two agencies – Cadw or the National Trust. It is said that if a historic property has a roof, then it is likely to be run by the National Trust; otherwise it is probably the responsibility of Cadw. Not an infallible guide, of course, but a helpful start.

Wales has more castles and fortifications for its area than anywhere else in Europe.

Wales has more castles and fortifications for its area than anywhere else in Europe. If you include every earthwork revealed by archaeological surveys and aerial photography, there are more than six hundred sites. Their number and variety reflect the nation's turbulent and fascinating history.

In prehistoric times, life was a constant struggle for survival against the elements and attack by others. The earliest inhabitants of Wales made stone tools and weapons, but their limited building abilities were mainly directed at ceremonial matters and the commemoration of their dead. Though primitive fortifications exist, they are not substantial.

The **Celtic tribes**, who lived throughout what we now call the UK and Ireland before the arrival of the **Romans**, were notoriously warlike. The landscape – especially coastal promontories and hilltops with good views – is peppered with the remains of their substantial forts.

Above: **Chirk Castle.** The last of the castles built by Edward I in his conquest of Wales, Chirk Castle has fantastic gardens and a stunning view over nine counties.

The Romans introduced a sophisticated network of forts, barracks, roads and ports to sustain their legions as they encountered the troublesome tribes of the region they called **Cambria**. Many indigenous **Celts** eventually saw the advantage of adopting Roman ways, and their pragmatic co-operation made possible the governance of this remote extremity of the empire.

When the Romans began pulling out of their distant province of Britannia towards the end of the 4th century, the power vacuum was filled by regional rulers who provided the inspiration for the legendary **King Arthur**, mentioned for the first time in an early Welsh poem and later idealised into a paragon of chivalry.

The Saxons conquered much of what is now England but found Wales and Scotland fiercely resistant. During the 8th century, the eponymous **King Offa of Mercia** ordered the building of his dyke, a low earthwork that marked the western limit of his ambition and recognised the separateness of Wales.

On the Welsh side of **Offa's Dyke**, regional kings and princes consolidated their rule. Their courts were usually peripatetic and their households – families, soldiers, servants, minstrels and poets – moved between several castles. Through war, treaty and marriage their territories began to coalesce into an emerging Welsh nation.

In 1039, **Gruffudd ap Llywelyn** became the first ruler of a united and independent Welsh nation that was organised upon a sophisticated legal and constitutional foundation. But this was not the best timing. Within a couple of decades of the arrival of **William the Conqueror** in 1066, the **Normans** had taken the lands and powers of the Welsh princes in much of south-eastern Wales and were extending their influence and building their solid castles throughout the lowlands.

In 1267, **Llywelyn ap Gruffudd** was recognised by **Henry III as Prince of Wales**, but this harmonious arrangement was also short-lived. The English king **Edward I**, who came to power in 1272, aimed to bring Wales and Scotland fully under his rule. He spent vast sums in building his 'iron ring' of castles around Gwynedd, from where Llywelyn mounted his campaigns to retain

Clockwise from top left:
Gwydir Castle interior and exterior. Regarded as the finest Tudor house in Wales, Gwydir Castle was once the home to Katheryn of Berain, cousin of Elizabeth I.
Caldey Abbey. Caldey has been home to various orders of monks since Celtic times. Today the picturesque monastery overlooks the pretty island cottages, Village Green and Shop.
Tenby Tudor Merchant's House. This late 15th century town house is furnished to recreate the atmosphere of family life in Tudor times.

independence. Having succeeded in securing solid support throughout Wales against overwhelming forces, Llywelyn was eventually ambushed and killed at Cilmeri near Builth Wells in 1282.

Numerous fortified mansions and grand homes in the style of medieval castles have been built in Wales since those distant days of strife, but the pinnacle of castle building for military purposes was in the time of Edward I. The remarkable architecture and ingenuity of four of his castles – **Caernarfon, Conwy, Harlech** and **Beaumaris** – built by Master James of St George, the French genius in such matters, has been recognised in their collective designation as a UNESCO World Heritage Site.

Until the mid-18th century, Wales was a largely rural nation where landowners enjoyed the resources to build fine houses, and agricultural workers and their families lived modestly. The coastline was dotted with small harbours where fishing was the main activity.

The largest structures were the castles, which had long since outlived their purpose, and the great religious buildings, including the ruins of medieval abbeys.

The Industrial Revolution rapidly transformed the working pattern, the economy, the built environment and the social fabric of Wales. Within a few decades,

small towns and villages were transformed into some of the largest concentrations of industry in the world.

Merthyr Tydfil became the world's largest iron-producing centre, making possible the building of the railways. A pall of noxious fumes over **Swansea** and **Llanelli** reflected their specialisation in the smelting of copper, tin and other metals. Large numbers of people flocked to Wales from England and further afield, to provide manpower for the new industries.

The mining of coal in the south Wales Valleys boomed to the point where, by the early 20th century, 250,000 men toiled underground and **Cardiff** became the world's largest coal-exporting port. By this time, the combined population of the mining towns of the south Wales Valleys was equivalent – in number and variety of origin – to that of an additional large city.

Previous page: **Conwy Castle.** The castle's well-preserved walls give visitors the opportunity to walk along the top portions of the castle towers and town walls.
Above left: **Caerphilly Castle.** The castle was a revolutionary masterpiece of 13th century military planning due to its immense size (1.2h) and its large-scale use of water for defence.
Above right: **Menai Bridge.** At the time it was completed, Thomas Telford's bridge was the largest suspension bridge in the world.

The slate quarries of north and mid Wales expanded to meet the demand for roofing material at home, in Europe and in north America. Seaports grew to handle the thriving trade in raw materials and goods – and, as the railway network grew, to serve the passenger traffic to and from Ireland. Manufacturing industry expanded, particularly in south-eastern and north-eastern Wales.

Many of the industrial buildings and structures that made this ferment of activity possible – along with the grand houses built on its wealth – may be visited today. These heritage sites provide a fascinating insight into the way the people of Wales lived and worked in times gone by.

Several sites of the National Museum Wales (please see overleaf) provide especially direct insights into the industries that were so significant in shaping the appearance of the land and the character of the people.

Above: **Basingwerk Abbey.** During the 13th century Anglo-Welsh wars, Basingwerk's sympathies lay with the English. It apparently suffered little, and by the later 15th century had become quite prosperous. It was dissolved in 1536.

Left: **Bodnant Garden.** Spanning some 80 acres, Bodnant Garden is one of the most beautiful gardens in the UK.

Museums and galleries throughout Wales

In addition to the National Museums, you will find that most towns have a museum or heritage centre dedicated to the extraordinary variety of life and culture to be found in this deeply fascinating part of the world.

As befits a nation with such a rich history and well-preserved material heritage, Wales has many excellent museums.

As befits a nation with such a rich history and well-preserved material heritage, Wales has many excellent museums.

The **National Museum Wales** is a widely dispersed group of leading institutions. The **National Slate Museum** in Llanberis, tells how the quarrymen extracted the versatile building and roofing material from the mountains, and describes their tough lives. The

National Wool Museum in the Teifi valley is the place to try carding and spinning for yourself, and to learn all about wool production and use.

Few museums offer anything quite as dramatic as the underground tour at the **Big Pit National Coal Museum** near Blaenavon. And few put information technology to such

Above left: **Oriel Mostyn Gallery.**
The Oriel Mostyn Gallery in Llandudno north Wales is one the UK's premier contemporary, modern and fine art galleries.
Above right: **National Museum Cardiff.** The National Museum Cardiff houses one of Europe's finest art collections as well as preserving some of the nation's treasures.

effective use as the **National Waterfront Museum** in Swansea, which tells the story of the people of Wales at work, in industries old and new.

St Fagans National History Museum is one of Europe's very best open-air museums, featuring a wonderful collection of buildings relocated from all over Wales, together with absorbing indoor exhibitions about rural life and folk traditions.

The **National Museum Cardiff** is the nation's storehouse of all that is best in many and varied fields of interest – from archaeology to zoology, decorative arts, fine art, geology, science, technology and many other areas.

In addition to the National Museums, you will find that most towns have a museum or heritage centre dedicated to the extraordinary variety of life and culture to be found in this deeply fascinating part of the world.

Interesting museums include the **Llangollen Motor Museum** and **Pendine Museum of Speed**, the **National Coracle Centre**, which displays coracles from all over the world, the **Rhondda Heritage Park** and the **Blaenavon World Heritage Museum**, a testimony to the pre-eminence of south Wales as the world's major producer of iron and coal in the 19th century.

Wales has a long tradition of artistic expression, which continues today. Many gifted

artists and craftspersons live and work here and their work is sold from galleries and studios across the land. Collections of fine art, from Wales and elsewhere, have been assembled both by the nation and by individual collectors.

Collections of fine art, from Wales and elsewhere, have been assembled both by the nation and by individual collectors.

National Museum Cardiff
displays many treasures including a significant collection of Impressionist works by Renoir, Monet and Cézanne. Eminent Welsh artists also feature, including 18th century landscape pioneers Richard Wilson and Thomas Jones, and 20th century artists Augustus John, Gwen John and Ceri Richards.

The **National Portrait Gallery** in Wales has over 100 portraits from the 19th century collections including works by John Singer Sargent and the Pre-Raphaelites.

The **Turner House Gallery** in Penarth shows fine art of the highest quality.

Above: **National Portrait Gallery.**
The National Portrait Gallery at Bodelwyddan Castle houses many wonderful portraits from the 19th century.

The westernmost regions of Wales (especially Anglesey, Snowdonia and Pembrokeshire) have inspired many artists. Look out for pleasing depictions of landscape, seascape, the seasons and rural life by Sir Kyffin Williams RA, William Selwyn, Rob Piercy, John Knapp-Fisher, Donald McIntyre and others.

Clusters of high-quality artists' studios may be found at Glynllifon (near Caernarfon), Ruthin, Hay-on-Wye and St Clears.

The biennial **Artes Mundi** competition at the **National Museum Cardiff** features the work of international conceptual artists.

Above left: **St Fagans.**
St Fagans Castle with its splendid Rose Garden is only one of many buildings you can explore in this informative open-air museum. Step back in time as far as the Iron Age and experience how Welsh people once lived and worked.

Above right: **National Waterfront Museum.** At the National Museum Wales's newest attraction you can experience noise, grime, high finance, upheaval, consumerism and opportunity and see how Wales's Industrial Revolution help shape the rest of the world.

Left: **Aberystwyth Arts Centre.**
The award-winning Aberystwyth Arts Centre has a wide-ranging programme of events and activities across all art forms. It is recognised as a national centre for arts development and welcomes over 650,000 visitors a year through their doors.

Festivals and events throughout Wales

There are festivals in Wales for just about every aspect of culture. You will find everything from large national events to local musical and literary festivals, carnivals, regattas and shows that draw the crowds to historic villages, towns and harbours.

You will find everything from large national events to local musical and literary festivals, carnivals, regattas and shows that draw the crowds to historic villages, towns and harbours.

The main tourism season in Wales extends from Easter onwards, through the summer, until the school term begins in early September. Countless events, suitable for all the family, are organised during these months. Many places also provide ample reason to visit throughout the year, by organising activities and entertainment appropriate to autumn, Christmas, and other times.

Above left: **Aberystwyth and Ceredigion County Show.** This County Show is one of many across Wales that promote agriculture and bring together the farming industry and the local community. Shows like these hold a number of events that make great days out for visitors.
Above right: **The Big Cheese, Caerphilly.** This is an annual celebration of local and Welsh heritage, history, culture and entertainment. The festival includes jugglers, fire eaters, living history re-enactments, music, funfair rides and more.

Musical, literary and theatrical enthusiasms feature strongly and you will find performances at every level from professional venue to village hall. The orchestra of **Welsh National Opera** and the **BBC National Orchestra of Wales** appear at spectacular open-air concerts each summer; at Swansea's Proms in the Park, Cardiff Bay and elsewhere.

Musical styles ranging from classical to brass bands, and from jazz to folk and roots music, have strong followings at festivals, halls and clubs across the land. Authentic Welsh folk traditions, including music and dance, are still celebrated, notably in and around Cardiff, at the beginning of May and at Christmas and New Year.

The traditions of the countryside are a recurrent theme, central to the identity of many Welsh people. Despite the demands of the farming life, the seasonal pattern allows time for the agricultural shows at local and national level. The largest of these, the **Royal Welsh Agricultural Show** is held at Builth Wells during **July**, with the **Winter Fair** following at the same venue early in **December**. Smaller shows, to which all are welcome, are organised at county level throughout Wales.

Some of the more vigorous, and occasionally dangerous, traditional sports have disappeared but Wales has made a unique contribution in this area

of endeavour. The little town of **Llanwrtyd Wells** has become famous for its calendar of what can only be described as profoundly wacky challenges, including the **world bog-snorkelling championships**! The latter requires an unusual ability to ignore the cold and unsavoury surroundings, and to navigate in zero visibility, as you swim as rapidly as you can for the finish line.

The largest annual events arrive one after the other during the spring, summer and early autumn. Typically organised by experienced professionals supported by resourceful local committees, they feature big names in their respective fields and provide a visitor experience second-to-none.

Llanwrtyd Wells has become famous for its world bog- snorkelling championships!

Above: **Welsh National Opera at Cardiff Bay.** The Oval Basin at Cardiff Bay hosts fabulous open-air concerts by big names, including Welsh National Opera, as well as being a venue for other events such as Cardiff's International Food and Drink Festival.

The Hay Festival of Literature, held each May, sees world-famous authors, and enthusiastic readers.

The **Hay Festival of Literature**, held each **May**, sees world-famous authors, and enthusiastic readers who appreciate a good book, congregating at the small town of Hay-on-Wye, which has more than 30 bookshops.

Brecon pulsates to the sounds of jazz during **August**, when traditional bands and skilled solo practitioners of the more rarified forms come to town for the **Brecon Jazz Festival**.

Bryn Terfel, the world's leading bass-baritone, invites world-class guests to join him on stage before an enthusiastic home audience at his annual **Faenol Festival** (voted Best Show in Wales) held near Bangor each **August** Bank Holiday.

The Cardiff Festival offers an exciting series of concerts throughout the summer.

The **Cardiff Festival** offers an exciting series of concerts, a multicultural carnival, a harbour festival, food shows, sports competitions and many other events throughout the summer, in the city centre and at Cardiff Bay.

Celebrations of food and produce, including the **Abergavenny Food Festival**, make a point of inviting local companies to provide the best possible food and drink – both home-produced and more exotic.

The largest of Wales's cultural festivals – in fact, one of the largest in Europe, with a daily attendance typically exceeding 20,000 – is the **National Eisteddfod**. This week-long gathering follows a tradition established by Lord Rhys at Cardigan Castle in 1176, whereby poets and musicians (and nowadays many other talented and creative participants) meet in a spirit of friendly competition.

Clockwise from top left:
Hay Literature Festival. This world-renowned literary festival hosts talks and book signings of the biggest names of the time. Authors from around the world come here to promote their new books. A must for book-lovers.
Brecon Jazz Festival. One of the best jazz festivals in Europe and all the tickets to see the big names performing will go fast. Even if you don't have a ticket, you can soak up the Festival's vibrant atmosphere.
Abergavenny Food Festival. Eagerly awaited by foodies, the Abergavenny Food Festival is one of the largest in the UK.

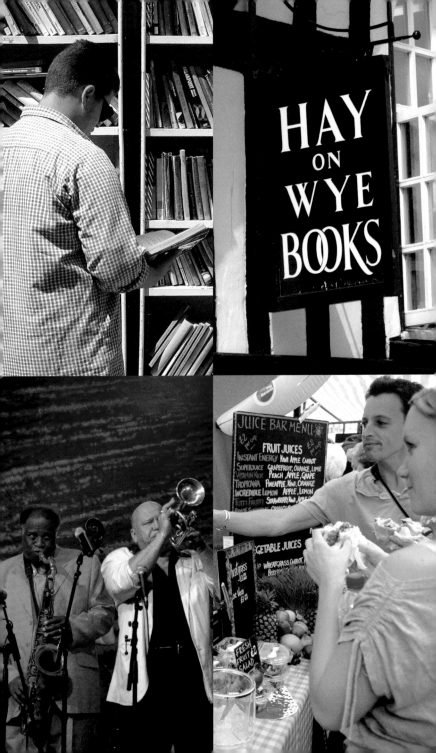

The largest of Wales's cultural festivals – in fact, one of the largest in Europe, with a daily attendance typically exceeding 20,000 – is the National Eisteddfod.

Held at the beginning of **August**, the **National Eisteddfod** moves to a different part of Wales each year. The enormous pavilion, venue for competitions and evening concerts, seats some 3,500 people. The surrounding Maes, or campus, has several smaller performance and exhibition spaces and upwards of 300 stands, where most of Wales's cultural and educational organisations are represented.

The central point of the **National Eisteddfod** is that everything happens in the Welsh language. Simultaneous-translation receivers are available at the main entrance and anyone wishing to learn the language will be made welcome at the Learners' Pavilion – there's a hotly contested prize for Welsh Learner of the Year.

The principle of friendly competition has been extended worldwide by the **Llangollen International Musical Eisteddfod**. This captivating multicultural gathering originated in 1947 as a means of bringing together like-

minded people from all over war-ravaged Europe. One of its most moving moments being the first appearance by a choir from Germany in 1949. Performers of appropriately high ability nowadays travel from all over the world to attend in a spirit of shared appreciation.

Performers of appropriately high ability nowadays travel from all over the world to attend in a spirit of shared appreciation.

Little wonder then, that this is the only festival in the world to have been nominated for the Nobel Peace Prize.

Above left: **Royal Welsh Show.** The Royal Welsh Show is one of the most prestigious events of its type in Europe, and brings to together the farming industry and rural community in a celebration of the best of British agriculture with a unique and very special 'Welsh' flavour.

Above right: **Cardiff Festival.** Cardiff Festival is the UK's largest free outdoor festival, and brings colour and cultural vibrancy to the city and the waterfront area of Cardiff Bay.

The Welsh language

The ancient language of Wales is very much alive during the 21st century and is spoken by around half a million people.

Welsh evolved from the Celtic languages spoken throughout Britain at the time of the Roman occupation. These included two distinct forms: the Goidelic group, which produced the Irish, Scots Gaelic and Manx (Isle of Man) languages, and the Brythonic group, from which the Welsh, Cornish and Breton languages emerged.

Welsh is one of Europe's oldest languages and is by far the strongest survivor of all the Celtic tongues. As with all languages, it has over many centuries absorbed words and influences from elsewhere.

There is no compulsion to speak Welsh but many people deeply enjoy doing so. The lyrical nature of the language seems designed to produce pleasingly poetic sounds and opens the door to a treasure trove of culture. Even the smallest attempt at learning the basics will be much appreciated by the people you meet, even if they need to help you a little with some of the pronunciation.

The language is generally phonetic, so that each letter represents only one sound: what is written is what you say. Some of the sounds however differ from English, as follows:

'a' as in 'apple'
'e' as in 'exit'
'i' as in 'ee'
'o' as in office
'u' sounds similar to the 'i' in 'win', but longer
'w' as in 'win' - serves as a vowel
'y' as the 'u' in 'cup', but longer – serves as a vowel
the famous 'll' is akin to the 'tl' sound in the English words 'antler' or 'Bentley'- but you breathe out gently as you say it.
the Welsh 'ch' is similar to that in Johann Sebastian Bach, a highly regarded figure in Wales!
'dd' sounds like the 'th' in then
'th' sounds like the 'th' in thing

Websites

www.bwrdd-yr-iaith.org.uk (information on the Welsh language)
www.bbc.co.uk/wales/learnwelsh

A few helpful words and phrases

Good morning	Bore da
Good afternoon	Prynhawn da
Goodbye	Hwyl fawr
Good evening	Noswaith dda
Good health!/Cheers	Iechyd da!
Good night	Nos da
How are you?	Sut mae?
Very good	Da iawn
Welcome	Croeso
Welcome to Wales	Croeso i Gymru
fine thanks	iawn diolch
yes	ie
no	na
please	os gwelwch yn dda
Thank you	Diolch
Good	Da
small	bach
big	mawr
where is?	ble mae?
castle	castell
river	afon
food	bwyd
drink	diod
I'd like a pint of...	Hoffwn i beint o...
And a glass of...	a gwydriad o...
Where am I?	Ble ydw i?
I'm lost!	Dwi ar goll!
Where's the nearest cashpoint?	Ble mae'r twll yn y wal agosaf?

Graffeg books

Graffeg publish illustrated books about contemporary life in Wales. Each book is focused on a particular interest: landscapes, food, lifestyle, heritage, architecture, festivals, music, arts, sports and culture. Graffeg books make wonderful guides, travelling companions and gifts.

View our catalogue online www.graffeg.com

Visit our website for the latest news and view the Graffeg book list online @ ww.graffeg.com Browse through books online before you order.

Published by Graffeg.
Tel: 029 2037 7312
sales@graffeg.com
www.graffeg.com

About the authors

Written by
David Williams

David Williams is a writer and photographer having a wide-ranging knowledge of the life, culture and history of Wales. He wrote, and supplied images for, the Graffeg books Landscape Wales, About Cardiff and About Wales – and for other titles in this series of pocket guides. He works for numerous book and magazine publishers, broadcasters, tourism authorities and cultural organisations. A graduate of the University of Wales, he is a fluent Welsh speaker.

As a contributor to Photolibrary Wales, his images help to promote Wales worldwide. Having travelled throughout Wales, he is thoroughly familiar with its people and places, and able to offer a balanced perspective on the whole of our compact but enormously fascinating nation.

Foreword by
Siân Lloyd

Originally from Neath, Siân Lloyd attended school in Ystalyfera and studied at the universities of Cardiff and Oxford. She worked as a television presenter with S4C, and as a radio and television journalist, before joining the ITV national weather team. She reports on the environment for ITN, and on travel and environmental matters for national newspapers.

Her wide spectrum of television appearances, as presenter and guest, includes children's programmes, quizzes, chat shows, talent shows, consumer programmes and current-affairs discussions. Her interests include food – cooking it, eating it, and writing and making programmes about it! – mountain walking (from Wales to the Alps), chess, Scrabble, films and theatre.

Index

Picture Credits
Copyright to all images contained in this book is represented by the following:
© **Crown Copyright**: 3, 16, 20, 21, 22, 24, 26, 29, 32, 48, 62, 74, 76, 82, 86, 88, 91, 95, 96, 97. **Cadw (Crown Copyright)**: 30, 80. **David Williams**: 6. © **Graham Lawrence/Alamy**: 46. **Janet Baxter**: 3, 56, 58, 65, 66, 67, 68, 90. © **Jeff Morgan/Alamy**: 18. **National Library Wales**: 52. **National Museum Cardiff**: 85. **National Waterfront Museum**: 89. © **NTPL/ Andreas von Eisiedel** 56. **Erik Pelham** 76. **Peter Gill & Associates**: 4, 40, 95. **Photolibrary Wales**: 8, 9, 12, 14, 31, 35, 36, 38, 43, 44, 50, 51, 54, 55, 60, 64, 76, 78, 81, 82, 84, 88, 92, 95. **Severn Trent Water**: 3, 39.